The Big Box

By Carmel Reilly

Here is Em.

Em has a big box
and a pen.

Zac is here, too.

Zac has a big box.

Zac can get into his box.

The box is a bus!

Zac sits in the box,
but Em can not fit!

Em looks at her box.

Is the box big?

Yes, the box is big!

Is the box a bus?

No, it is not a bus ...

Em gets a cap.

She sits in her box.

Zac gets in, too.

The box is a big jet!

Em and Zac zip
up, up, up!

CHECKING FOR MEANING

1. What did Zac make with his box? *(Literal)*

2. Why didn't Em get in Zac's bus? *(Literal)*

3. What was the pen used for in the story? *(Inferential)*

EXTENDING VOCABULARY

box	How many sounds are in this word? What are they? If you take away the letter *b* and put another letter at the start, what new word can you make?
Yes	What is the opposite of the word *yes*? What other words do you know that are opposites of each other? E.g. day – night; hot – cold; big – little; short – tall.
zip	What does *zip* mean in this story? Does it have only one meaning? How else can you use this word?

MOVING BEYOND THE TEXT

1. If you had a big box, what would you make? Why?

2. What would you draw with the pen?

3. What is your favourite toy? Where did you get it?

4. Describe what your favourite toy looks like.

SPEED SOUNDS

Xx	Yy	Zz

Kk	Ll	Vv	Qq	Ww

Dd	Jj	Oo	Gg	Uu

Cc	Bb	Rr	Ee	Ff	Hh	Nn

Mm	Ss	Aa	Pp	Ii	Tt

PRACTICE WORDS

box

Yes

Zac

zip

Zip